Perspectives on Passing the Bar Exam: How We Did It, and How You Can, Too!

AF808102

By

Peter L. Brewer, Esq.
Sabrina C. Call, Esq.
Bernard S. Klosowski, Jr., Esq.
John M. Rappold, Esq.,
and
Jeremy M. Stipkala, Esq.

To you, Dear Reader:
May You Pass The Bar Exam!

Published by Persimmon Woods Press, LLC

eBook ISBN 978-0-9997997-4-1

Paperback Book ISBN 978-0-9997997-5-8

Table of Contents

I. Jeremy's Introduction

Here we go, Dear Reader! It is time to start studying for the bar exam!

You are probably flush with joyful confidence as you graduate from law school: you have mastered a new, practical, prestigious, stimulating, and wonderful area of human knowledge and endeavor, **The Law**. Yet that confidence is tinged with a shadow of anxiety about the upcoming bar exam. If you do not pass the bar exam, all you will have is a nice diploma to hang on the wall and so much legal knowledge that makes you a walking civics course. Oh yeah, and a ton of student debt. If you think about it too much, that anxiety will blossom into raw fear and ruin your day. At the furthest periphery of your mind lurks the awful question that no-one dares whisper aloud, *"What if I do not pass the bar exam?"*

Fear not, Dear Reader! On the pages that follow, a diverse group of attorneys relate their bar exam experiences. They range from those who passed on the first try, to those who needed multiple attempts and endured *years* of that anxious question gnawing at their minds. We have attorneys who took bar exams in multiple jurisdictions, and another who can compare The Old Format with the Uniform Bar Exam. Each attorney prepared for the bar exam differently. Some attorneys studied full-time, while others studied while working a job. Significantly, we believe that the life circumstances surrounding our bar exam success stories will resonate with different segments of our audience. That's you, Dear Reader. We have captured here what each of those attorneys, if they could jump into a time machine, would tell their younger selves about **what worked for them to pass the bar exam.**

We sincerely hope that you find much that is useful. Significantly, we wrote this book for two kinds of attorney candidates: those who want to pass on their **first attempt**, and those who want to pass on their *very next* attempt. Several wonderful bar preparation courses teach the substance of the law tested on the bar exam. However, given the *thousands and thousands* of attorney candidates who fail each year, there must be something missing from those attorney candidates' preparation. We offer our insight with the aspiration that you, Dear Reader, *do not have to take the bar exam again.*

This diverse group of attorneys has two things in common. First, we all passed the bar exam. Second, we each care very deeply about the attorney candidates who follow in our footsteps. So please read on. We look forward to you joining us in that extraordinarily marvelous endeavor, **the licensed practice of law**.

II. Peter's Thoughts on Passing the Bar Examination

By Peter L. Brewer, Esq.

A. "Absolutely American"

Several years ago, I read a book called "Absolutely American." The book was written by a Rolling Stones writer, and followed students at West Point as they moved through the process of becoming commissioned officers. The writer was granted unusual access to the military academy, and was able to interview and follow individual students during their careers at West Point. One thing that stood out to me was that every cadet had his or her own unique motivation for going through the grueling process.

For many their motivation was pure patriotism – they wanted to become Rangers or they wanted to fly helicopters or they wanted to be in the Corps of Engineers

– they wanted to serve. For others, it was the opportunity for a free education, and little more. For others, it was a stepping stone for a later career on Wall Street or in business. Whatever the driving force, the ones who made it through were the ones who kept their focus on the end goal without getting discouraged by the endless challenges and obstacles presented at West Point.

One of those challenges is that each cadet is intentionally given more tasks each day than they can handle, or at least excel at. This means that each cadet has to make a decision daily as to what is most important, knowing that many other things must receive less attention.

B. What Is Most Important?

The bar examination is the same way. Regardless of their motive for wanting to become a lawyer, the law school graduate must create a plan and stick to it. He or she must decide each day, based on the plan, what is most important for that day. One can only spend so much time on criminal procedure, knowing that there are many other topics that need to be addressed. Therefore, my advice is to read what you can, memorize what you can, and move on. Do not succumb to the temptation of going back and studying yesterday's outlines and notes, because then you will miss today's information.

Studying for the bar exam is like eating an elephant – it can be eaten only one bite at a time. The amount of material is overwhelming, but if you plan your time in advance, you can take those bites in manageable quantities, and perhaps even come back to chew those same bites again right before the test. Stay focused on the ultimate goal, and do not let yourself become discouraged because you can't master it all.

We have all heard stories of individuals who went to law school, then took the bar exam, and failed. And they took the exam a second time and still did not pass. There are two reasons for this – either they did not establish a base of legal knowledge while they were in law school, and now it is simply too late, or they did establish a proper base but they did not respect the test enough to adequately study before sitting for the bar. Assuming that you actually attended classes in law school and made an effort to learn the material, you should have acquired the knowledge and skills needed to pass the bar, and pass it the first time. Now you have to create the time – two to three months of your life – and dedicate yourself to intense daily study.

You must create a calendar setting out what you will study each day. Follow the calendar, read the outlines, and make outlines of the outlines. In this digital world there is still no better way to learn material than to write it down. And once you have done that, trust your instincts; trust your base of knowledge you have; and trust your ability to recall information. You will do fine.

Do not be lulled into a false sense of security based on your performance in law school. I know a law review editor that failed the first time, and I know people who were at the bottom of their law school class who did very well taking the bar. The key, again, is respecting the test and studying daily.

C. "How Do You Spell That Name Again?"

My first year out of law school I was fortunate enough to be selected to serve as a Brief Attorney at the Texas Supreme Court. One of the jobs of the supreme court is to oversee the Board of Law Examiners in Texas, and to "bless" the results of the examination when they come in. This also means that the very first people to actually see the test results and to know who passed are the staff working at the court. Law school graduates know this and make it a point to find out who the Briefing Attorneys are going in.

Shortly after the test results came in, the phones in my office started ringing. It was my friends, and friends of my friends, and even people I did not know, calling in to ask, "Is my name on the list?" It was always a joy to tell someone that they had passed and that their years of hard work had paid off. (I confess that it was also a joy to toy with them by asking them to spell their name several times, and dragging out my "search process" by a few extra moments.) But it was terribly difficult to tell someone that their name was not found, and they will have to try again, or maybe there was an administrative issue that just needs to be remedied.

You know the statistics – you know that most students pass on the first try. If you respect the test and study diligently, disciplining yourself to follow your calendar as you go, your odds are very high that you will be fine.

III. How Sabrina Studied for and Passed the South Carolina Bar Exam

By Sabrina C. Call, Esq.

A. Introduction

During law school I knew eventually I would have to take the bar exam, but it was not something I was worried about in the least. At that time, I was solely focused on the classes I was taking and the exams I had to pass in order to graduate from law school. I just assumed passing the bar exam would happen magically after graduating, and I would move into the next phase of my life. My lackadaisical attitude is one of the big reasons why I did not pass the bar exam on my first try. Let me paint a picture for you of my first attempt.

In January 2014, I was in my 3L year of law school and I had just started working a new part-time job. On top of that, I got engaged on New Year's Eve. So, newly engaged and employed, I was thrilled with the way life was going. I was counting down the days until I would graduate and finally enter the "real world."

A few weeks after graduating in May 2014, I began studying for the July bar exam using a nationally recognized bar prep course online. I had signed up for this bar prep course at the beginning of my 1L year. I remember these companies had tables set up in our library advertising their services. If I signed up for the course, I could pay a portion of the cost each year during law school instead of paying for the whole thing at the end. It sounded like a great plan to me, so I signed up.

Once I was nearing the home stretch of law school, my professors and bar prep advisors all recommended that students STOP working if we had a job, postpone planning anything big like a wedding (my fiancé and I had decided to get married in September, a mere six weeks after the bar exam), and treat studying as a full-time job. I did the exact opposite.

I decided to keep my part-time job so I would have at least a little bit of money coming in and I knew I would be glad to have the job once the bar exam was over. When I wasn't working, I was studying at home. The bar prep course I had chosen provided me with a schedule to follow from May through July. Each day would focus on a specific topic, and they spelled out exactly what I should try to accomplish each day in order to cover all of the material by exam day.

This all sounds well and good, but in reality, the daily expectations for this course seemed outrageous. I had already fallen behind after the first few days. I tried telling myself that maybe that was normal. Maybe the expectations for this course were purposely set higher than necessary just to motivate people and keep them feeling a sense of urgency. I had heard from other bar studiers that "no one" was able to keep up with the course expectations, so that helped me feel okay with my progress.

B. Study Techniques for Bar Exam Number One

The study materials included with my bar prep course included online video lectures for all of the different subjects with a handy fill-in-the-blank book to use as you watched the lectures. This book was actually very helpful and helped me stay focused as I watched the lectures.

I did have the option of going to a classroom each day with other bar studiers, but this option did not suit me at all. I tried this method one day and then never went back. The day I arrived I saw a classroom full of people in my same situation. After a few minutes someone came in and pushed "play" on the lecture video. I was a bit baffled. What was the point in me driving downtown to watch a video when I could stay at home and watch the same video? At home, I could press pause, I could rewind the video if I ever missed something, or I could take a break and eat if I got hungry. There seemed to be no benefit to me sitting in a classroom while watching the video lecture, so I was done with that.

Along with the video lectures, my study materials also included countless practice essays, countless practice MBE questions and numerous practice exams of various lengths.

I remember I watched all of the video lectures, even the ones that were painstakingly boring. I completed some of the practice MBE questions, some of the practice essays and a couple of the full-length practice exams. I do not remember the number of essays or questions available to me, but I can assure you I did not complete all of them. I also did not keep track of the number of practice MBE questions I completed, nor did I keep track of the number of essays or practice exams I completed. I was unbelievably slack with my studying. Mentally I still did not appreciate how difficult the bar exam was going to be.

I do, however, remember buying nearly a million white index cards. I spent hours upon hours creating flash cards, and I guarantee I spent 90% more time making the flash cards than actually using them. I told myself that making them was good practice since I had to read the law and write it out, but this was a terrible plan for me. If you can make flash cards quickly in the beginning, and then actually use them to study during the couple of months leading up to the exam, then by all means go right ahead. It may be helpful for you, but the way I did it was not. I'm pretty sure I was just trying to distract myself, subconsciously, from actually having to study.

C. Distractions, Distractions

I am not blaming her, let me just get that out of the way. But on top of everything my Mom called, texted or emailed me just about every day. She would think of things that needed to be done to prepare for the wedding (coming up in September) and wanted to discuss them with me. This is completely normal, but I really wasn't interested in planning the wedding. I wanted to get married, but I just wanted someone to tell me when to show up and I would be there. My Mom's stress about the wedding did not help my state of mind for studying.

If I could go back in time, obviously I would not turn down the proposal. My husband and I were destined to be together. I wouldn't change the time of year we got married either. The only thing I would do differently would be to skip taking that first July bar exam. It was a complete waste of my time, money and energy since I was trying to juggle too many things at once and I did not give the bar exam the attention and priority that it deserved.

If I had waited until after our wedding, I could have applied for the February bar exam and had one less (huge) thing on my plate while studying. Throughout law school, it was always my plan to graduate and then take the exam. It never occurred to me to postpone taking the bar exam. If I had waited, another six months would have gone by and I still wouldn't be an attorney. Being impatient is part of my personality, so that is unfortunately not something that I could change.

My Advice Tip #1 – If you have too many things going on in your life when you are planning to take the bar exam, JUST WAIT. There will be another chance for you to take the exam in a few months, so be patient.

D. Marathon Training

Another thing you cannot fully appreciate until you've taken the bar exam is the physical toll this exam will take on your body. This cannot be understated. You obviously have to train your mind to be prepared for the exam of a lifetime, but if you aren't physically prepared as well, then you really will start to notice it after the first section or two of the exam. It sounds weak to complain about sitting in a chair for three days, but your body isn't used to it so you need to train your body and increase your stamina and endurance.

To prepare, you have to make yourself get exercise while you are studying and eat healthy. Figure out a routine that works for you. I've always preferred exercising first thing in the morning, so that's what I did. After studying for hours, if I needed a break I would go for a walk outside or go swimming to get some more exercise and sunshine. Having a head full of legal knowledge is great, but if your body starts to feel drained and tired, then you are not going to be able to recall all of that knowledge when you need it the most during the exam. It truly is like training for a marathon, mentally and physically.

E. Location, Location, Location

The South Carolina bar exam is held two times each year in Columbia, South Carolina. Columbia is my home town, so I stayed at my Mom's house during my first bar exam instead of getting a hotel room. Each of the three exam mornings I would get up, drive downtown, find a parking spot in the garage and go inside to take the exam.

After the exam each day I would drive the twenty minutes back to my Mom's house and eat dinner with my family. I do not remember studying much, if at all, after the exam because all of my energy was completely drained. Staying with my Mom seemed like the most logical plan. At the time, it didn't make sense for me to get a hotel room when I had a perfectly good room waiting at my Mom's house. When that first bar exam was finally over, I had no idea if I had done well or not. I had no feeling of confidence or impending doom. Everything just felt like a blur and mentally, and probably physically, I had my fingers crossed.

I failed this first exam, and afterwards I decided I had to do things completely differently for my second attempt. That following February I stayed in a hotel right across from the Convention Center where the bar exam is held. This time I still went out to eat with my family each night after each day of the exam, but I did review some of the study materials at the end of each day. Doing away with that morning commute did relieve some of my stress. Being able to sleep an extra ten minutes and then just walk across the street for the exam was great. I highly recommend getting a hotel room to anyone who is planning to take the bar exam. And make sure to book it early, because the hotels will fill up quickly.

After failing my second exam, I knew I had to change things drastically for my third attempt. That following July, for my third bar exam attempt, I stayed in a hotel across from the Convention Center again, but this time I did not see my family while I was in town. I hibernated in my room, I ate dinner in my room and I studied the whole time when I wasn't taking the exam. I was constantly reviewing notes or study material and I was totally in the zone this time. And it worked!

F. Pulling Yourself Together After Failing

When the bar exam is over, you feel a bit of relief, but then you realize you have to wait two or three months before the results are released. You have to get back on track in the real world, whether you want to or not. Just because you've been in bar prep mode does not mean your bills stop coming.

After each bar exam, I immediately went looking for a new job. After the first bar exam, I was fortunate and found a full-time job as a legal assistant with a local law firm that needed my help "at least through the end of November." They were preparing for a murder trial, and needed someone who could stay with the firm at least through the end of the trial. I wasn't planning to go into criminal law as a career, but this sounded like a really great opportunity to me since I needed to be working, but would hopefully pass the bar exam in a few months and then be looking for a full-time attorney position in a different field.

Everything was going well until October when I learned I had not passed the bar exam. I was at work when I got the results, and I could not have been more devastated.

My Advice Tip #2 – Do not get the bar exam results while you are at work, if you can help it. If you don't pass, you will feel devastated and you won't want to be around other people. I wish I could have been at home when the results were posted.

I'm sure many people, after they learn they haven't passed, will want to drink themselves into oblivion. That is somewhat understandable, but I didn't do that. I probably had a drink that night, but nothing remarkable. I knew, as devastated as I was, that my next step would be to STOP WORKING, completely this time, and study full-time for the February bar exam. I was worried about what my husband was going to think about my plan. I hated to tell him I was going to be putting my life on pause for the next three months and not bringing any money in, but I knew I had to be selfish about this. Luckily my husband was very understanding. So, I worked a few more weeks at my job and then left on good terms. I ordered my next round of study materials, applied for the February bar exam, and started studying.

I did not pass the second exam either, but I was much, much closer. When the second exam was over, I knew I needed to find another job. This time I worked for a really wonderful financial institution in town. I have amazing memories from that job, and

I still keep in touch with the people I met there. I have even received client referrals from this company. For many reasons, I count that experience as one of the best in my life.

When the exam results came out a few months later, I learned again that I had not passed the bar exam. I had improved by leaps and bounds, though, and was much closer to passing. This time I planned ahead and was at home when I got my results, just to be on the safe side.

I hated to think I had to stop working again, but that's what I did. I stopped working and focused full time, again, on studying for my third bar exam.

G. What Worked for My Preparation?

My efforts preparing for my third and final bar exam were different than in the past. This time I kept track of every single thing I was doing. I answered over 2000 MBE prep questions, which I believe was the key to me passing the MBE. That seemed to be the magic number because at that point I felt like that the questions start repeating themselves in different ways, and my brain already had most of them memorized. This is the frame of mind you want to be in when you head in to take the MBE. Your brain should almost be on autopilot. You don't want to have to reread any questions; you want to be able to breeze through a question and know what they're going to ask before you get to the end of the question. Your brain should be so familiar with these questions that you anticipate your answer before you're finished reading.

You should try to feel the same way with the essay questions. This third time, I answered all of the essay questions for each subject (or at least outlined them). Try to complete as many of the practice essays for each subject as you possibly can. Answering these questions over and over again really is the only way for your brain to learn.

I also was really fortunate because I had another attorney who was gracious enough to act as my tutor (Jeremy, co-author of this book). He reviewed many of my essays and afterwards we went over the essays together. He was also there to offer unending moral support during those times I didn't pass the exam.

I did numerous timed essays. I think these timed essays are a really great way to prepare you for the pace of the exams. You need to be familiar with the speed you'll be expected to work at on exam day, and what better way to prepare than to actually put yourself in a similar timed situation?

I also recommend getting out in the sunshine! I would go sit by the pool and review study material from time to time just to get out of my apartment. As I mentioned before, going for a walk outside was a great way to get blood flowing and helped break up the monotony and tedium of studying hour after hour.

H. What Worked on the Bar Exam Itself?

Skipping around during essays was a TREMENDOUS help to me! I cannot stress this enough. It was something that I only decided to do on this last and final time I took the bar exam, and I fully believed it is what enabled me to pass. But be very careful to write your essays in the correct places!

My Advice Tip #3 – Briefly review the essay questions presented to you, and then choose the one you know the most about. Answer the questions in your preferred order. This will keep your brain juices flowing and you'll have more to write about (meaning more points!).

During my third attempt, I even had time to stop, go to the restroom, get a sip of water, and review my essays with time to spare. I had never felt this way in the past and I am telling you, this is the way you SHOULD feel when you have confidently answered all of the essays proficiently.

The MBE questions also became much easier on my third attempt. By this last exam, my brain had memorized so many of these questions and I could spot the issues almost instantly. My brain had memorized little variations in the questions too so I could spot exactly what the question was asking instead of being tricked.

I. Final Word

Don't be slack like I was for my first attempt. Everyone will tell you to take the bar exam seriously, and you really do have to listen to them. Start studying as soon as possible. If there is a bar prep course you can take in law school, take it. Go ahead and start preparing slowly during your last semester of law school. Once school ends and you graduate, kick everything into high gear and start studying immediately.

Postpone any big plans if possible, set your bills up on auto-pay, and tell your friends and family you will see them again in three months. Study like you've never studied before. Stick to a schedule and force yourself to repeat things over and over again. Find a tutor who is willing to review your essays or quiz you with flash cards. If study groups help you, then find a good study group.

Always remember though, if you don't pass on your first attempt, don't give up. Many, many people have failed bar exams over the years and then gone on to be successful. Just to name a few: Michelle Obama, Hillary Clinton, John F. Kennedy, Jr. and even former Associate Justice of the United States Supreme Court Benjamin N. Cardozo. You just have to pick yourself up and try again. You can't let this one exam derail what you spent years of your life building.

IV. How Ben Passed Four Bar Exams – While Working!

By Ben Klosowski, Esq.

A. Commitment and Routine

How? Commitment and routine. I looked at each bar exam as my job for about eight weeks.

Yes, the title above sounds braggadocios. But if you survived college and law school, you, too, are sufficiently intelligent and resourceful to prepare for and pass a bar exam. The difference that I discovered between some of my unsuccessful peers and me was commitment. I viewed the bar exam as my job so that I could get and keep another job -- in a law firm, eventually. I noticed that some of my peers, on the other hand, treated the bar exam as a part-time endeavor and continued to pour much of their energy into things like, ironically, the non-legal job they were in at that time. I'm not saying cheat your current employer – if you have a job – while you prepare for the bar exam; I'm just saying the bar exam must be your first love. For eight weeks, at least.

My first bar preparation and exam was in Maryland in the summer of 1998 while I was working full-time as a program manager for a systems engineering firm (a 45-minute commute each way, too), serving in the U.S. Navy Reserves once a month (sometimes two weekends a month), and my wife and I also were raising a 3-year old daughter, all with a baby boy on the way! A busy schedule, as I recall....

So, I decided after graduation from law school in the spring of 1998 – having sacrificed the preceding few years in law school – that I needed to treat the bar exam as my most important job during the eight-to-twelve weeks leading up to the exam for two reasons: first, why spend all those years and money on law school if I wasn't going to pass the bar exam; and second, I wanted to start a legal career, not to continue doing what I was doing – that was the whole point, right?

I decided that I could hold my breath and do anything for eight weeks. Why not pass the bar exam on the first try? (I have a friend who required six attempts to pass the Virginia bar. Another friend gave up after four tries. I did not want to endure that fate.)

Next, after commitment, came routine. For me, I set aside two hours every morning to practice bar exam questions and write essays. I spotted issues, made up and memorized mnemonics (I still use many of them in practice to this day!), and forced myself to actually write down answers/essays. No fooling myself with "thinking" about the answers. I would then grade my essays, literally with a red pen. If I came up with a new mnemonic or pointer, I would add it to a "Summary Sheet" that I was keeping on the side. (Keep your Summary Sheet simple. The Summary Sheet is for glancing at the evening before the bar exam, maybe the morning of. If you've recreated a "Horn Book," it will make your eyes glaze over and you might panic.

A one-page (no more than two pages) of bullet points will serve to refresh your memory and give you confidence.) Then I would go to work and take care of other responsibilities during the day. In the evening, after dinner, I would spend another hour or two working on more practice exams. I repeated the routine on Saturday and Sunday, too. After about one week, the routine became routine. It went on like that for a couple of months and finally the bar exam day arrived. The only thing I glanced over the morning of the exam was my Summary Sheet.

There are many courses, test preparation materials, and suggestions for getting us to the bar exam, so I won't delve into those, but I found that the "muscle memory" of practicing tests and writing out answers every day served me well on the day of the bar exam. This is because I was on automatic pilot - 90% of the answers jumped out at me despite being nervous, and the other 10% of the questions that were more difficult or unclear, I confidently reasoned my way through. I was confident, or calm I guess, because I knew I had nailed the bulk of the questions and essays quickly and efficiently thereby creating some breathing room for myself for the harder questions.

B. No Resting on My Laurels

I was admitted to the Maryland bar on June 24, 1999. But I didn't rest on my laurels. I wanted admission to the D.C. bar due in part to the geography and in part to the type of practice I wanted to have. Rumor at the time had it that the D.C. bar was "easy." (That's what everybody said, anyway.) Ignore such rumors. That's like kids in school talking about Old Man Smith's 5th period algebra exam – live by those rumors, die by them. So, I jumped in feet first and practiced intensely for the few weeks preceding the D.C. bar. (Notice I say, "practice" not "study" – we studied in law school. The bar exam isn't really about learning or "studying" new law; it's about practicing exams.) I did, in fact, find the D.C. bar relatively easy, not because of the content but probably because I took it on the heels of the Maryland bar and the law was fresh in my mind and because I again had committed to it with a practical practice routine. I was admitted to the D.C. bar in November 2000, first try.

This brings me to an important observation. Bar exams are artificial in that they are testing us to recall myriad laws in an absurdly compressed amount of time. If anyone practiced law under bar exam conditions, that lawyer would probably be sued for malpractice. However, bar exam preparation did instill "issue spotting" skills in me that I still use to help me begin taking apart client problems. In other words, the rote issue-spotting tool that I developed during bar preparation helps me focus to this day. Clients are paying us lawyers for our time so an efficient start can't be beat. But as an old law partner told me when a client demanded an answer immediately, "Tell him that we're on the 16th floor and there is no drive through service here!"

Turning back to my bar exam adventures, an old Navy buddy-now lawyer and I had exchanged Christmas greetings in 1999. My friend asked me to consider joining his firm in South Carolina because they needed "patent attorneys." I had the technical background to become federally registered as a patent attorney, but that would mean taking not one but two more bar exams!

Well, I interviewed with a different South Carolina intellectual property law firm in the spring of 2000, was offered a position, and joined that firm in July 2000. As expected, this meant preparing for and taking the patent bar in order to be admitted to practice before the United States Patent and Trademark Office. Beyond that, looming large on the horizon, was the South Carolina bar. Well, one thing at a time....

C. Oh, Those Squinty Looks!

There I was, Naval Officer, engineering program manager, now junior associate in a patent boutique firm. All that leadership and program management expertise, law school theory, and bar exam experience? Of some help, but knowing the law and applying it on clients' behalf?

Those are kinda different things in the real world. So, much of the work that the firm was giving to me in the beginning was light boilerplate stuff, or I was combing through piles of discovery documents looking for smoking guns – not quite the stuff of bar exam essays. In the meantime, though the firm was saying "bill bill bill," one of the partners fortunately pulled me aside and said, "Do what you can billing-wise but focus on the patent bar." Hmm. Sounded like my old mantra – commitment to the job of passing the bar exam.

So, for six weeks, while at work, if I had nothing urgent to do, I'd close the door and practice patent bar exams. I even came in a couple of hours late for a few weeks. I figured that someone would say something if I was really off-base, and yes, I got a few squinty looks from partners and associates alike, but I hung on to that partner's words to focus on the patent bar exam. That partner also said that in the long run no one would care about a few months of light billing from me (since I didn't have much practical billable experience anyway!); that they'd be happier down the road if I passed the patent bar. I did. The October 2000 patent bar national pass rate was less than 40%. What made the difference, I believe, was when I decided that the firm was paying me to become a patent attorney; that the patent bar was my temporary, primary job.

Another associate who had been hired a few months before me was a star in our firm – he had had practical experience as a patent examiner before becoming an attorney. His billing was terrific, and he was making the firm some money! Problem was, he didn't pass the patent bar with me in October 2000. He didn't pass it again six months later. A few months after that, the firm cut him loose. I eventually was selected for partnership. I think I made the right choice to focus on the patent bar.

One more thing. Right after the patent bar, I had to turn around and study for the South Carolina bar. Commitment and routine to the rescue again. I endured a few (less squinty) looks for a few weeks and passed the South Carolina bar on the first try and was admitted in November 2001. I then turned my full attention to serving my clients, and I was offered partnership about six years later.

I've been in practice for nearly twenty years now. I don't expect to have to sit for another bar exam. However, if I ever do, I will fully embrace Bar Exam preparation once again – I will make it my job, develop a routine – build muscle memory, and hold my breath for eight weeks!

Good luck!

V. A Not So Brief (But Useful!) History of John's Bar Exam Experiences

By John M. Rappold, Esq.

A. How Could This Happen to Me?

After failing the South Carolina Bar three times, I was about to give up. Nothing in my life, at least academically, had ever been so frustrating. I attended the Charleston School of Law and graduated with a respectable "B" average. I was even able to do so without exerting much more effort than I had in college, while attending the College of Charleston. I also heard that many of my classmates, who I used to study with and who, on occasion, would come to me for help with law school finals, also passed the Bar. As such, I told myself (and truly believed) that the Bar was unlikely to give me much trouble. As long as I put in the time and stayed focused, I would be walking out of that exam room with an air of confidence and an audacious smile. However, this was not my fate.

After graduating from law school in December, 2014, I decided to take the July, 2015 Bar, rather than the February, 2015 Bar. This decision was primarily prompted by a number of family matters requiring my attention, but was also made to ensure that I would pass the Bar on my first try. With seven whole months available to me now, I could wrap up any remaining familial concerns by April, still have plenty of time to swoop in and out of this bastard test, and never look back. I wasn't going to rush with only two months of preparation, only to be back in July anyway, like a lot of those suckers. I was going to buckle down and be overly prepared, with at least three months to do so.

I began with what most of my classmates and most law school graduates do, deciding whether to enroll in a Barbri® or Kaplan® Bar prep course. I had heard that Barbri® was "better," though more expensive. So, my sights were set on Barbri®. However, as is my nature, I phoned both companies a number of times to get the price down. They actually got into a bit of a bidding war, to my surprise, in order to secure me as their student. I won't digress much further, but do recommend that all students try this, as I was able to secure my Barbri® Bar prep class for about 60 percent of their listed price.

Before I knew it, I was going to the Barbri® class and spending much of my time outside of class doing what they told me to do, following their study plan. Though I put in roughly six hours per day, as opposed to the eight to ten they recommended, I felt pretty good (at least as prepared as one can sanely feel) about taking the Bar by the end of July. It was a three-day exam, consisting of two, six-hour days of essay testing and a third, six-hour day of the multiple-choice Multistate Bar Exam. I would be lying to you if I said I felt confident that I had passed the Bar when I walked out of that testing room. However, because I knew most of the answers to the questions asked and the substantive law required to answer them, I did feel my odds were…favorable. As it turned out, I did quite well on the Multistate Bar Exam, scoring a 125. This was the exact, minimum score that was required on the SC Bar, in order to be allowed to fail one essay section. Welp, I failed two… and by only a few points each. While this was frustrating, it was also encouraging. Call me a "glass is half-full" kinda guy, but failing by only a few measly points was better than being way off the mark. So, no problem here. "I'll get it next time." Right?...WRONG.

Fortunately (in my mind), Barbri® allowed any student who had taken their class but was unsuccessful on the Bar to take advantage of the same resources up until the immediately following Bar. So, after a sigh of resignation and anguish, I began going through the motions again, watching Barbri® lectures online, completing practice essays, doing practice multiple-choice questions to stay fresh on those, etc. It sucked… But I was sure that going through all of this again, after coming so close to passing on my first attempt, would surely result in a passing score this time around. I must know what I'm doing, or at least be going about this thing largely in the right

way, to have come so close.
Right?...WRONG AGAIN!

By the end of February (the time of my second Bar Exam) I felt I had picked up any and all loose pieces of the law that I may have missed before and was more prepared than anyone had ever been for any Bar...EVER! Perhaps... overly prepared. At the hotel I booked in Columbia, SC, the day before the Bar were full of countless flashcards, sample essays, and several outlines covering the same areas of law, some self-created and others from peers. As dusk came around, I was feeling pretty good and was ready to relax for a few hours before a solid night's sleep. I mean, I had done much more to prepare for this Bar than the first one, and had studied as much as one can. So, I'll be good...right? I hate to do this again, but...WRONG. I ran into a serious problem that night. I could not sleep a wink. My brain was spinning with everything I had studied over the past several weeks and especially the voluminous amount of material I had brought along and reviewed that day. I literally laid in bed from about 11pm until about 4am without any success in getting to sleep. So, I said, "#%*& it! I'll just get up, continue studying, and make sure that this unfortunate mishap doesn't screw things up for me today." This was a bad idea. Obviously, I felt horrible during the first day of the Bar. That night, I wasn't able to get more than 20 minutes of review in before falling asleep with a Civil Procedure outline strewn across my chest.

My results showed that I had failed two-thirds of the essays on BOTH DAYS! I was already pissed by what had happened before I got my results, but this made it official. Even so, every section I failed was not up to snuff by less than 10 points. I felt that I had actually put too much time and energy into this Bar, so much so that I was getting tunnel vision and letting it consume me.

For my third attempt, I did my best to keep myself busy with other tasks. I began working as a law clerk at a personal injury firm in North Charleston, SC. It provided me with a great deal of practical experience and the pay, though not substantial, took a bit of the "this could be the end of the world" edge off the Bar. This time, I felt that if I just did what I had to prepare the first time, PLUS get some sleep during the nights of the Bar, I would pass. I had the whole firm rooting for me and my boss even helped me with my essay writing.

You are probably sick of hearing about my relentless trying and failing fight with the Bar and want me to get on to the good stuff. What allowed me to pass? The next few sentences are arguably the most important in this chapter. In preparation for my third time taking the SC Bar, I studied how I had the first time when I very nearly passed. I knew the substantive law better than ever before and was able to retrieve it more readily. I felt calm, collected, and, yes, was able to sleep decently well the nights leading up to and during the Bar. Alas, I failed again.

"WHAT HAPPENED?," you ask? Yes, by this time I was able to score about a 150 on the MBE but, like my first go around, I failed two out of six essay sections by just a few points each. So, the approach I believed had to work, did not work. No matter how close to the goal I came, I still had not passed: my approach failed. If I was ever going to pass this thing, something had to change, dramatically. Now… ON TO THE GOOD STUFF!

B. The Good Stuff

For my fourth attempt at passing the SC Bar, I discarded most of my earlier Bar prep materials and took a new approach.

The third time I took the SC Bar was the last time they administered the awful three-day format, before converting to the two-day Uniform Bar Exam format. In light of this change, I thought it would be prudent to take a second Bar prep class, geared toward success on this new format. As Barbri® had not worked for me in the past, and Kaplan® was cheaper, I decided to go with Kaplan®. While I am glad that I did, it was much like Barbri®. This time, however, I didn't follow it so closely. I allowed it to familiarize me with the new (at least new to me) Uniform Bar Exam format, but did not allow it to carve out my study schedule. Of course, much (if not most) of Kaplan®'s teachings were great, and I did prefer their less-produced, less-cheesy presentation, when compared to Barbri®. However, this was not my first rodeo and I had seen it all before.

When I began preparing for the Uniform Bar Exam, I knew three things:

1) I did not need help on the Multistate Bar Exam (doing as many practice questions as you can is most effective and, in my opinion, is the best and only way to study for it);

2) I needed to find a way to effectively answer essay questions without getting bogged down in details or peripheral matters, which steals away precious time and also precious points.

3) I needed to make sure that I addressed essay questions clearly and methodically.

Interestingly, even at this point, I couldn't be entirely sure whether I was coming up short because I was actually missing the thrust of the question, or because I wasn't effectively/clearly/logically/lawyerly communicating my essentially-correct answer. Yes, I know we are all taught in law school to spell out our analysis, as if we were explaining it to a child or our grandmother. "A, in that B. B, in that C. C, in that D"… The stress of the Bar can be overwhelming and make anyone forget their "training" and rush from B to D. Was that my issue? Or was I simply addressing minor (and wrong) issues instead of the major issue? At that time, a lot of my previous Bar experience seemed a blur to me, so there was no point in trying to decipher exactly what made my answers inadequate. Today was a new day. This was a new (fourth) chance. This was a fresh start with a new Bar. Right?...RIGHT!

C. What Made It Happen/The Time It Worked/Feeling Like Rudy

First: I committed to doing 20-25 multiple-choice questions every day. I took comfort in the fact that, as long as I did 20-25 multiple-choice questions per-day (tops), I would have the entire second day, and half the Bar Exam, in the bag.

Second: Early in my preparation, I leisurely read thought the comprehensive Kaplan® outlines once. This gave me more context than I needed and made me feel like a bit of a "know it all" by the time I moved on to shorter outlines. Then, I selected the best outlines I had for each subject, and jettisoned the rest of the crap I used on the previous Bars. By "best" I mean the outlines that meshed well with Kaplan®'s comprehensive outlines, focused on the typically litigated/major issues, and ultimately made me feel the most confident to answer an essay question on the subject. So, I separated these outlines from the others, stuck with them, and never looked back. Frequently, these were the shortest outlines, like Kaplan®'s attack outlines, or another 10-15 page outline depending on the subject, but NEVER more than 20 pages. You simply do not need and will have a hard time internalizing more information than this when considering how rapidly you'll have to whip it out on the Bar. Keep in mind I am talking about subjects, like Wills, and not sections, like Wills, Trusts, and Estates. Having two outlines for each subject made me feel more secure and confident that I was not missing something (at least nothing big). In contrast, I knew that reading the same words, in the exact same order, over and over again from a single outline on a subject, my brain would eventually read the words without absorbing them. I would use these outlines to internalize the law by reviewing at least a section's worth of them every day.

Third: I watched Kaplan® lecture videos. Some would say that watching the Kaplan® lectures was not the most effective use of my time, and I might agree. However, it was nice (and I might say beneficial) to take a break, in a way, from the intense attack outline studying/practice essay writing. As with much in life, diversification is key and can actually make studying easier on your brain by keeping it interested and engaged, rather than trying to force it to be. However, I say this with caution. Too much diversification can be just that, too much. Figure out the two or three things that work best for you. If you're not sure, go with what makes you feel the most confident and willing to take on a practice essay after you're done with it. Throw everything else away! Actually, just keep it out of sight and mind, in case you need to look something up it might contain.

Fourth: I wrote practice essays. After I had spent a week or two reviewing pretty much what I already knew, aside from a few and far between "ah…I did not know that" moments, I immediately started doing practice essays. Not as many as I could get my hands on, necessarily, but enough to keep me busy for a couple of hours after reading through my two chosen, and now "two and only," outlines for each subject. I did this once a day, every day, for the thirty days leading up to the Bar, no more than two or three subjects in any one day. I did the subjects together that would be tested together, like Wills, Trusts, and Estates. Remember, this was my FOURTH time studying essentially the same material. It is okay if you're still learning the substantive law by the time you start doing practice essays. Please do start exposing yourself to them more than thirty days before the exam. Just get a good base going in your brain for each subject that you can hopefully call on to give you some confidence. And, if you're like me, the ones you miss will end up being the ones that stick, so stride on.

D. The Big Picture

If I had to say what caused me to fail the Bar three times, or what enabled me to finally conquer it in the end, the answer would be the same: 1) Practice, 2) Practice, and 3) Practice. It goes without saying, but learning the substantive law is a requirement to pass any state's Bar Exam. Memorization, though not the key, is important, and one of many keys required to unlock the complex, multi-deadlock door to admission. However, I believe learning and memorizing the substantive law to be only about 20% of the fight. What grants you entry is practice. Practice allows you to learn how to put down into your own clear effective words what you have spent so much time and energy learning from the beginning. But don't reserve practice for the home stretch, just a few days before the Bar. Instead, practice early and often. This was something I goofed up on at least my first attempt, and probably my second.

Practice multiple-choice and essay questions under timed conditions to make sure you are managing your time well. Practice to probe whether you have insufficient knowledge of black-letter law. If you do lack knowledge, go back to the two outlines you've chosen to represent that area of the law and try again. Peeking at your outlines during practice essay questions is ok early in your study, but you won't be able to manage your time properly if you still have to late in your preparation, and you certainly won't be allowed to peek at your outlines during the exam. Make the practice experience a realistic experience.

Practice to make sure that you are answering the call of each and every question. It is easy to allow issues that initially jump off the page at you to cloud your mind and distract you from what the question is really asking.

Practice to make sure that your answers address and discuss a substantial amount of the same issues that the sample answers do. Your answers and the sample answers do not have to match, and rarely do. But make sure that you don't check it off the list when the sample answer really elaborates on an issue and you barely manage to mention that issue in passing. The point is to address the issues that will earn you the most points, while leaving peripheral, smaller point-grabs for time you might have left over. If time runs short, just address the peripheral issues in a few words. This will enable the grader to give you a couple more points if you need them. Your discussion of the peripheral issues might never be read if you earn enough points to pass that essay by spending your time and words where you should, on the big-point issues.

Finally, practice to give yourself confidence and calm. No matter how secure you may feel from studying the hell out of your outlines and doing a practice essay here and there, everything changes when you walk into that room on Exam Day. The "Oh $#%^, I should have done more practice essays" feeling might hit you if you don't practice. Don't do that to yourself! It's hard to get going on them and easy to call it "good" after doing a handful on each subject. But for as much material you have to study for each section being tested, the actual questions asked typically only account for and relate to about one-fourth to one-third of that material. I can't even count the number of times I went back to my hotel room after a day of essay testing and went through my notecards or outlines in search of an answer I was unsure about, only to repeatedly say to myself, "Wow, that wasn't on the Bar…Nope, neither was any of this…I can't believe they didn't ask anything about [insert huge and 'typically tested' area of the law here]." It sucks that you have to study "everything" when this is true, but completing dozens of practice essays enables you to see several different approaches the test writers might take in assessing your knowledge. Even when I felt comfortable and was, in fact, very knowledgeable in an area of the law, I would find practice essays really helping me demonstrate that. Don't let a lack of experience with practice essays prevent you from recognizing the context in which a law or set of laws may be addressed and really sticking it to those graders. There is nothing worse than walking out of an essay exam and overhearing someone talking about an area you know inside and out but did not discuss because you failed to recognize its applicability to the fact pattern. I have been there and it takes time to forgive yourself for it.

E. My Final Note: The Bar Exam Is Not Hard

I understand that I may seem crazy saying it, after how damn "hard" it was for me. But please, hear me out.... When I say that the Bar is not hard, I mean, it's not *that* hard. If you've graduated from law school, no matter what law school you attended and no matter if you had an A or a C average, I am confident that you can pass this thing. To touch on something I mentioned earlier, I can't count the number of my fellow law school graduates, who routinely came to me for help in law school, who passed the bar well before I did. I wasn't a straight-A student...but these were straight-C students! At first, I couldn't make sense of it. I could not believe it. How could this be? Luck? No. While there are times you may get lucky on the Bar exam, this is no True or False test. My point is…don't let yourself make this into something more than it is: a bunch of softball law school essays, all crammed into one long, exhausting endurance race. The challenge is not the difficulty of the questions, or even the amount of substantive law to which it pertains. It's keeping your cool, trusting yourself, and managing your time. It's like completing a bunch of law school essays, in the classes you got As to Cs on (hopefully), and only having to explain yourself enough to achieve a D on them. How hard can that be?

VI. Jeremy's Final Word of Encouragement

Such a diversity of experiences reveals a few key points, and many helpful details. Peter stresses discerning what is most important, and maintaining the discipline to grasp it each day. Sabrina emphasizes focus, excluding life's distractions and postponing your bar exam if you cannot. Ben presents commitment and routine as his keys to succeeding on the bar exam, showing that it is possible to prepare even while working. John's dogged determination to pass the bar exam taught him the importance of practicing and the destructive futility of cramming.

The details matter too. Creating outlines of excruciating complexity, or flash cards for that matter, do not offer a primary or universal method for passing the bar exam. **Practice**, for a few hours before and after work, for example, and early in your preparation, appears **essential**. Timed practice under realistic testing conditions builds the mind and body (and hands and butt) to tackle each question with vigor and to go the distance during two or three days of examination. And it helps to pit bar preparation companies against each other, so you can get the lowest price possible.

We see what does not work. Underestimating the bar exam means that you, too, will become an expert at retaking the bar exam. Studying, to the exclusion of practicing, does not train you to write bar exam essays or to answer multiple-choice questions.

I am most inspired by my co-authors who had to commit to retaking the bar exam after failing. Overcoming the mental anguish, self-doubt, and dejection of missing the mark by a little or by a lot, to climb that mountain again – and to **triumph** – should inspire and encourage you, Dear Reader. John's and Sabrina's perseverance shows me that they have the Right Stuff to be attorneys, too, because we will all face setbacks and defeats in our careers. It comes with the territory. Helping our clients as zealous advocates means that we put our "all" into our cases. When we lose, it hurts bad. But just like John and Sabrina, we have to pick ourselves up and Get Back On That Horse, because our clients need our help. That is why the phones keep ringing, and the e-mail messages keep coming. (Ben and Peter, taking multiple bar exams, well that's just nuts – who does that?) (Well I did that, too. Perhaps *I am* nuts. Hahahahaha!)

We hope these diverse tales inspire and encourage you as you prepare for your bar exam. If you need a day-by-day bar preparation calendar and concrete guidance on how to address essay questions, practical tests, and multiple-choice questions, please check out my book, "Pass the Bar Exam with Dr. Stipkala's Proven Method," available in hard copy and e-book. If you have feedback, questions, or comments, we want to hear from you. Kindly e-mail us at DrStipkala@gmail.com, or do a Google® internet search for us and reach us at our law practices. And we want to hear your victory speech, Counselor!

Made in the USA
Monee, IL
04 November 2026

67385559R00036